# ROLL OF HONOUR

OF

## MEMBERS OF THE SOCIETY OF WRITERS TO HIS MAJESTY'S SIGNET, AND APPRENTICES

1914-1919

Printed by
WILLIAM BLACKWOOD AND SONS
EDINBURGH AND LONDON

# Roll of Honour

OF

## MEMBERS OF THE SOCIETY OF WRITERS TO HIS MAJESTY'S SIGNET, AND APPRENTICES.

### 1914-1919.

2ND LIEUTENANT ROBERT ADAMSON, 98 Irish Street, Dumfries.

Enlisted November 1914 in 18th Royal Fusiliers (1st Public School's Battalion). Received Commission 27th September 1916, 3rd Battalion King's Own Scottish Borderers. Served in France November 1915 to May 1916, and January 1917 to July 1917. Discharged September 1917 on account of ill-health contracted on Active Service.

CAPTAIN EDWARD MURRAY MAYNE ALEXANDER, 6 Darnaway Street, Edinburgh.

Enlisted in November 1914. Received Commission as 1st Lieutenant 30th November 1914, and as Captain 20th December 1914, Seaforth Highlanders. Served in France May to July 1916, and October 1917 to April 1918. Wounded (Somme) 14th July 1916. Wounded, losing leg, Wytschaete, 16th April 1918.

LIEUTENANT GAVIN LEITH ALLARDYCE, M.C., 122 George Street, Edinburgh.

Enlisted 2nd Honourable Artillery Company Infantry May 1915. Received Commission, 2nd Lieutenant 7th Gordon Highlanders, December 1916. Served at Battle of Arras, April 1917; Third Battle of Ypres, July 1917; First Battle of Cambrai, November-December 1917; Second Battle of Somme, March 1918; Second Battle of Cambrai, October 1918. Twice wounded. Taken prisoner 20th October 1918. Awarded Military Cross.

MAJOR CHARLES ANDERSON, D.S.O., M.C., Glenburn Hall, Jedburgh.

Enlisted as Trooper in 1st Lovat Scouts September 1914. Received Commission in 15th Royal Scots January 1915. Served in France and Belgium from January 1916 to February 1919. Awarded D.S.O. and M.C. Mentioned in Dispatches.

**LIEUTENANT ROBERT BALLANTINE ANDERSON,** Glenburn Hall, Jedburgh.

Enlisted as Trooper in 1st Lovat Scouts September 1914. Received Commission King's Own Scottish Borderers January 1915. Served in Gallipoli July 1915 till evacuation. Thereafter in Egypt and Palestine. Killed in action on 19th April 1917, at Gaza, Palestine.

2ND LIEUTENANT HENRY VANS ANDERSON, Glenburn Hall, Jedburgh. (Apprentice.)

Gazetted 2nd Lieutenant 141st Heavy Battery Royal Garrison Artillery January 1918. Served in France until date of demobilisation.

CAPTAIN THE HON. JAMES MONCREIFF BALFOUR, O.B.E., 16 Charlotte Square, Edinburgh.

Received Commission as 2nd Lieutenant Scottish Horse August 1914. Promoted Captain October 1914 and Staff Captain in 1915. Attached to 3rd Echelon G.H.Q., France, 1916-17. War Office 1917. Assistant Secretary Ministry of National Service 1917-18. Awarded O.B.E. (Military Division) 1919.

LIEUTENANT JOHN MACKINTOSH BELL, Mansfield, Moffat.

Received Commission as 2nd Lieutenant 5th King's Own Scottish Borderers on 10th September 1915. Thereafter promoted Lieutenant. Served at home until 8th March 1919.

LIEUT.-COLONEL LEWIS LEONARD BILTON, C.M.G., 17 Rutland Street, Edinburgh.

Received Commission as 2nd Lieutenant Army Service Corps September 1914. Posted to 17th Battalion The Royal Scots, of which Second in command. Transferred to 2/8th Battalion The Worcestershire Regiment, which he commanded from July 1916. Temporary command of Brigade January-March 1918. Served abroad from August 1915 to June 1918. Promoted Lieut.-Colonel. Instructor at Senior Officers' School Aldershot July 1918. Awarded C.M.G. Croix de Guerre Belgique. Twice mentioned in Dispatches.

LIEUTENANT COLIN MACKENZIE BLACK, 28 Castle Street, Edinburgh.

Received Commission as 2nd Lieutenant King's Royal Rifle Corps in December 1915. Promoted Lieutenant. Thereafter A.D.C. and Camp Commandant Headquarters 39th Division B.E.F. Served in France from September to December 1917. Discharged in January 1918.

LIEUTENANT THOMAS WILSON BLACK, 42 Lancaster Gate, London, W. 2. (Apprentice.)

Gazetted 2nd Lieutenant in 1st Battalion 1st Lowland Heavy Battery 4th March 1915. Served in this country until July 1916. Promoted Lieutenant. Served abroad until May 1917.

LIEUTENANT WILLIAM BLACK, 36 Castle Street, Edinburgh.

Enlisted in Mechanical Transport Royal Army Service Corps May 1916. Served nine months with the Salonica Forces. Received Commission 10th September 1917. Afterwards served in France.

MAJOR WILLIAM THORBURN BLACKWOOD, M.C., British Linen Bank, Peebles.

Enlisted in Inns of Court Officers' Training Corps in December 1915. Received Commission in Royal Scots January 1917. Served in 8th Royal Scots (Pioneers) in France from February 1917 till April 1918. Seconded for duty as Adjutant and Assistant Commandant, thereafter Major Commanding 51st (H) Divisional Reception Camp, France, June 1918. Awarded M.C.

LIEUT.-COLONEL ALEXANDER STEVENSON BLAIR, C.M.G., T.D., 12 South Charlotte Street, Edinburgh.

Lieut.-Colonel 9th Royal Scots. Mobilised 4th August 1914. Commanded the Battalion in France from February 1915 till May 1916. Commandant (Temporary Colonel) commanding Abancourt Area Lines of Communication from May 1916 to December 1917. Awarded C.M.G. Twice mentioned in Dispatches 1916 and 1917. T.D. 1918.

LIEUTENANT ARCHIBALD BLAIR, 28 Charlotte Square, Edinburgh.

Enlisted 8th Royal Scots September 1914. Received Commission as 2nd Lieutenant September 1914 and Lieutenant June 1915. Relinquished Commission December 1916 as result of accident in France. Re-commissioned Lieutenant Royal Field Corps (afterwards Royal Air Force) May 1917. Served at home and abroad. Wounded 16th May 1915.

CAPTAIN JOHN JAMES BONAR, 3 St Margaret's Road, Edinburgh. (Apprentice.)

Gazetted 2nd Lieutenant 19th November 1914. Posted to 6th Royal Scots and attached to Tank Corps from 3rd January 1918. Served in this country and in France until 25th January 1919. Promoted Captain.

**CAPTAIN JAMES DONALDSON BOSWALL,** of Wardie, Midlothian and Haartebeeslehock Farm, Pretoria, Transvaal.

Enlisted in 9th Royal Scots in September 1914. Commissioned as Captain in January 1915 in 10th Battalion Seaforth Highlanders. Thereafter attached to 1st Battalion the Essex Regiment. Served in Gallipoli, and was killed in action 6th June 1915.

LIEUT.-COLONEL JOHN DOUGLAS BOSWELL, Garrallan, Cumnock, Ayrshire.

Mobilised 4th August 1914 as Lieut.-Colonel Commanding Ayrshire Yeomanry 1914-15 on Coast Defences. Proceeded to Gallipoli September 1915, where till evacuation. Thereafter in Egypt, where took part in Battles of Katta and Romani; and afterwards put in Command of the 12th (Ayr and Lanark Yeomanry) Battalion Royal Scots Fusiliers; with whom proceeded in March 1917 to Palestine and took part in Battles of Gaza. Holds Serbian Order of White Eagle.

**JOHN MACKENZIE BOW.**

Enlisted in Canadian Forces. Killed in action on 15th August 1917.

**LIEUT.-COLONEL ALEXANDER BROOK,** Haddington.

Mobilised 4th August 1914 as Major in 8th Royal Scots. Promoted Lieut.-Colonel and proceeded to France on 2nd November 1914 in command of his Battalion. Killed in Action May 1915. Mentioned in Dispatches.

**LIEUTENANT ARCHIBALD CAMPBELL BROWN,** "Faragon," Murrayfield, Edinburgh.

Commissioned as 2nd Lieutenant Royal Field Artillery in December 1915. Served in France with A 95 Battery Royal Field Artillery from 2nd September 1916 till 27th May 1918. Promoted Lieutenant August 1917. Killed on 27th May 1918 at Berry-au-Bac on the Aisne.

CAPTAIN CHARLES MARSHALL BROWN, 5 Thistle Street, Edinburgh. (Apprentice.)

Joined Royal Fusiliers (Sportsmans' Battalion) 8th October 1914. Gazetted 2nd Lieutenant 3rd Gordon Highlanders 9th November 1914. Promoted Captain. Served in this country and in France. Wounded at Hooge 25th September 1915 and at Paschendaele 26th September 1917.

**CAPTAIN WILLIAM SANDILANDS BROWN,** The Manse, Bellahouston, Glasgow, and 23 Ainslie Place, Edinburgh. (Apprentice.)

Enlisted in 15th Royal Scots September 1914. Gazetted 2nd Lieutenant 3rd North Staffordshire Regiment April 1915. Promoted Captain. Served in this country September 1914 until February 1916, and in France and Flanders from February 1916 until October 1918. Killed in action in Flanders 14th October 1918 when attached to 1/5th King's Own Scottish Borderers.

LIEUTENANT ARTHUR NICOL BRUCE, 10 Coates Gardens, Edinburgh.

Received Commission as 2nd Lieutenant in 7th Royal Scots in August 1915. Afterwards attached to Argyll and Sutherland Highlanders, Gordon Highlanders, and Seaforth Highlanders. Served in France in 1916 and N.W. Frontier India 1917-18. Promoted Lieutenant. Discharged through disablement from Service abroad February 1919.

MAJOR JAMES BRUCE, 16 Hill Street, Edinburgh.

Called up as Captain with Lowland Mounted Brigade Army Service Corps August 1914. Served at Dardanelles from September 1915 to January 1916, and from that date till July 1916 in Egypt. Also served with the Italian Expeditionary Force from December 1917 till January 1919. Promoted Major. Twice mentioned in Dispatches.

LIEUTENANT JOSEPH BUDGE, M.C., Easter Rarichie, Nigg, Ross-shire.

Enlisted as Trooper in Lovat Scouts in August 1915. Received Commission as 2nd Lieutenant in December 1915. Left for France December 1916. Served with Cameron Highlanders as Platoon Commander (1st Lieutenant) from January 1917 till May 1918. Afterwards attached to 1st French Mortar Battery as Section Commander. Awarded Military Cross (immediate award).

LIEUTENANT RONALD BURNESS, 12 Hope Street, Edinburgh.

Enlisted in Lothians and Border Horse in September 1914. Received Commission. Served with Lovat Scouts Yeomanry in Egypt from December 1915 till October 1916. In Macedonia (Salonica Field Force) from October 1916 till June 1918, and in France and Belgium from June 1918 onwards.

LIEUTENANT ALEXANDER BURN-MURDOCH, 140 Princes Street, Edinburgh.

Received Commission as 2nd Lieutenant 8th Royal Scots 9th March 1915. In May of that year became Machine-Gun Officer and later M.G. Instructor. In July 1915 went to France for duty at Base Depot until August 1915. Invalided at Stobs Camp May 1916. In June 1917 served as Signalling Instructor in Ireland till finally invalided in October of same year.

**RICHARD MORRIS BURNS,** 105 Dalkeith Road, Edinburgh.

Enlisted in 2nd Battalion Royal Scots Fusiliers in August 1914. Went to France in November 1914, and was killed at Neuve Chapelle on 11th March 1915.

CAPTAIN WILLIAM BURNS, 35 High Street, Hawick. (Apprentice.)

Mobilised in August 1914 as 2nd Lieutenant the Royal Scots. Adjutant August 1916 till August 1917. Served abroad from November 1917 till December 1917, and from September 1918 onwards. Promoted Captain.

MAJOR HEW FRANCIS CADELL, 21 Ainslie Place, Edinburgh.

Mobilised in August 1914 as Major in Lothian and Border Horse. Served with V. Corps Cavalry Regiment, Queen's Own Worcestershire Yeomanry, and Anzac Mounted Division. In France with the B.E.F. for eighteen months. Invalided. Served with the Egyptian Expeditionary Force for one year. Again invalided.

ACTING CAPTAIN ALEXANDER GORDON CAIRNS, 13 Hill Street, Edinburgh.

Enlisted as Trooper in Lothian and Border Horse in September 1914. Received Commission as 2nd Lieutenant Royal Field Artillery in February 1915. Served in France with 32nd Brigade Royal Field Artillery in 1915, 1916, and 1918. (Adjutant 1915-16). Invalided 1916 and 1919.

**2nd LIEUTENANT GEORGE MORTON CAIRNS,** 27 Buckingham Terrace, Edinburgh.

Enlisted in Army Service Corps M.T. in June 1915. Received Commission in Royal Highlanders (Black Watch) in December 1915. Went to France in September 1916, and was killed in action at Beaumont Hamel 13th November 1916.

LIEUTENANT JAMES ALEXANDER CAMERON, 5 Hill Street.

Received Commission as Lieutenant (General List) on 14th July 1917. Acted as Assistant Recruiting Staff Officer in Edinburgh till December 1917. Transferred to Staff of Ministry of National Service till 31st January 1919.

LIEUTENANT ARTHUR THOMAS CAMPBELL, Romanno, West Linton, Peeblesshire. (Apprentice.)

Gazetted 2nd Lieutenant Leicestershire Yeomanry and attached to 16th and 12th Lancers. Served in this country until 8th February 1916, and in France from that date until 21st September 1919. Promoted Acting Captain.

LIEUTENANT JOHN DOUGLAS-BOSWELL CAMPBELL, 25 Ainslie Place, Edinburgh.

Received Commission as Lieutenant in 1914 in Remount Depot Scottish Command. Assistant Commandant Remount Department, Ayr, from October 1914 till November 1915. Attached to Reserve Brigade Royal Field Artillery November till March 1916, when transferred to Royal Horse Artillery B.E.F. From March 1917 R.A. Instructor 6 "C" Reserve Brigade Royal Field Artillery.

**MAJOR ROBERT GILLIES CAMPBELL,** Crosby Buildings, Crosby Square, London.

Rejoined 10th Battalion Seaforth Highlanders in August 1914. Stationed at Cromarty from November 1914, and died at Cromarty on 1st February 1915.

**MAJOR HARRY CHEYNE,** 9 Hill Street, Edinburgh.

Mobilised as Lieutenant in 1st Lowland Brigade, Royal Field Artillery, in August 1914. Went to France with B.E.F. in October 1915. Promoted Major, and latterly in command of Battery. Was killed in action 10th July 1917.

MAJOR WILLIAM LESLIE CHRISTIE, 98 Hanover Street, Edinburgh.

Received Commission as 2nd Lieutenant Royal Garrison Artillery in November 1914. Served in France in August 1915 and from 29th May 1916 onwards. Promoted Major.

CAPTAIN THOMAS WILFRID BENNET CLARK, 11 Charlotte Square, Edinburgh.

Mobilised as Lieutenant in 9th Battalion Highlanders The Royal Scots in August 1914. Served in Belgium and France from February 1915 till July 1915, March 1916 till August 1916, February 1917 till April 1917, and from July 1918 till March 1919. Served at 2nd Battle of Ypres 1915, Battle of the Somme 1916, Battle of Arras 1917, and Battle of Soissons 1918. Wounded (Gassed) at the Somme in July 1916. Attached to 11th Battalion The Royal Scots British Army of the Rhine from March 1919 till November 1919.

2ND LIEUTENANT CHARLES GIBSON CONNELL, St Helier's, Lygon Road, Edinburgh. (Apprentice.)

Served in this country as Cadet in Royal Field Artillery from April 1917 until July 1918. Received Commission. Served in Salonica from August 1918 until February 1919.

LIEUTENANT HUGH HERBERT CONSIDINE, 2 Queen Street, Edinburgh.

Received Commission as 2nd Lieutenant in Royal Garrison Artillery, Special Reserve, in November 1915. Went to France in March 1916 with 38th Heavy Battery R.G.A. Engaged in Battles of Beaumont Hamel October 1916, Arras, Vimy Ridge, and Monchy, April 1917. Attack on Hindenburg Line at Bullecourt May 1917, 3rd Battle of Ypres, Pilken Ridge and Langemark, August and September 1917. Promoted Lieutenant June 1917. Invalided home in September 1917. Retired List April 1919.

CAPTAIN ADRIAN HENRY COOK, 22 Eglinton Crescent, Edinburgh.

Gazetted 2nd Lieutenant in 11th Battalion Argyll and Sutherland Highlanders. Served in this country and in France until April 1919. Promoted Captain. Twice mentioned in Dispatches.

2ND LIEUTENANT ALFRED WILLIAM HOWDEN COOPER, U.F. High Church Manse, Inverness. (Apprentice.)

Joined Inns of Court O.T.C, Lincoln's Inn, as Cadet, December 1914. Received Commission as 2nd Lieutenant 4th Battalion Cameron Highlanders April 1915. Served in France October 1915 to 4th April 1916, when invalided home. After service for one year at various Home Stations, returned to France March 1917. Severely wounded at Ypres on 31st July 1917. Thereafter served in different garrison towns in Ireland until February 1918.

CAPTAIN JAMES MURRAY COOPER, 42 St Albans Road, Edinburgh.

Received Commission as 2nd Lieutenant Royal Garrison Artillery in April 1915. Promoted Lieutenant July 1916 and Captain July 1917. Served in France from December 1916 till October 1917, when invalided home in consequence of Trench Fever and slight gas poisoning.

**CAPTAIN WILLIAM DERMOT COOPER,** 54 Manor Place, Edinburgh. (Apprentice.)

Mobilised in August 1914. Lieutenant in Ayrshire Yeomanry, and later attached to Royal Scots Fusiliers. Served in Gallipoli from September 1915 till evacuation, and afterwards in Egypt and Palestine. Wounded in advance to Palestine and killed in action near Gaza on 30th August 1917. Promoted Captain. Mentioned in Dispatches.

**MAJOR GEORGE DEAS COWAN,** 30 Dick Place, Edinburgh.

Mobilised in August 1914. Then Captain 9th Royal Scots. Went to France in February 1915. Promoted Major in June 1916. Killed in action 22nd April 1918. Mentioned in Dispatches.

CHARLES NEAVES COWPER, 18 Young Street, Edinburgh.

Mobilised 21st December 1916. Served in Royal Garrison Artillery, and was on the staff of Headquarters Office of the Siege Artillery Signalling Depot, Southamption and Fareham, Hants.

2ND LIEUTENANT CHARLES THOMAS COX, c/o G. H. Boyd, 16 Charlotte Square, Edinburgh.

Received Commission as 2nd Lieutenant Gordon Highlanders 20th July 1915. Passed to Reserve as 2nd Lieutenant 20th November 1916.

LAWRENCE JOHN CRAIGIE, Edenkerry, Broomieknowe, Midlothian.

Served as Private from 25th October 1916 in 2nd Royal Scots and thereafter transferred to 9th Black Watch.

LIEUTENANT JAMES BOWSTEAD CRAIK, 86 Inverleith Place, Edinburgh.

Received Commission in Royal Naval Volunteer Reserve in September 1915. Served in Command of H.M. Drifter, "Fisher Lassie II.," H.M. M.L. 267 and H.M. Drifter "Fizzer." Engaged in working Anti-Submarine Indicator nets and in protection of Fishing Fleet on East Coast.

LIEUTENANT ALASTAIR HENRY CRERAR, 11 Greenhill Place, Edinburgh. (Apprentice.)

Gazetted 2nd Lieutenant 9th Battalion Royal Scots Fusiliers 8th January 1916. Served in this country. Thereafter served abroad with 2nd Battalion Royal Scots Fusiliers. Wounded 12th October 1916. Thereafter attached to Royal Air Force.

WILLIAM CUMMING, 50 George Street, Edinburgh.

Served in this country from August 1917 as Gunner with the 2/1st Warwick (Heavy Battery) Royal Garrison Artillery, and in France from 11th October 1918 onwards as Signaller, afterwards as L.-Bombardier with 142nd Durham Heavy Battery Royal Garrison Artillery.

CAPTAIN ROBERT JEFFREY CUNNINGHAM, The Glint, Annan, Dumfriesshire.

Mobilised with 5th King's Own Scottish Borderers at outbreak of War. Served with Battalion on Coast Defence until April 1915, thereafter as Officer Commanding Regimental Depot Dumfries, until return of Battalion in October 1919.

CAPTAIN FREDERICK ROUS NEWLYN CURLE, Melrose.

Received Commission as 2nd Lieutenant Lanarkshire Yeomanry in December 1914. Went to France in December 1917 and invalided home with Trench Fever. Afterwards employed as Reconstruction Officer Scottish Command.

2ND LIEUTENANT RONALD KER CUTHBERTSON, 12 Church Hill, Edinburgh. (Apprentice.)

Served in Edinburgh University O.T.C. Thereafter with Royal Garrison Artillery at Brighton.

JAMES SANDERSON DALZIEL, Tigh-na-Traigh, Aberfoyle.

Joined 172nd Rocky Mountain Rangers Canadian Expeditionary Force in 1916, and after training in Canada was sent to this country. Owing to ill-health was not sent abroad.

MAJOR ROBERT STORMONTH-DARLING, Kelso.

Commissioned as 2nd Lieutenant Lothians and Border Horse in March 1915. Temporary Captain June 1915 to August 1916. Temporary Major August 1916. Went to France in April 1918 as A.D.C. to G.O.C 51st Division B.E.F.

LIEUTENANT P. FURNEAUX DAWSON, 23 York Place, Edinburgh.

Joined Royal Garrison Artillery as a Gunner in October 1916. Served in this country. Received Commission as 2nd Lieutenant 1st October 1917. Promoted Lieutenant 1st April 1919.

DAVID DEAS DEWAR, 6 Cornwall Road, Bedford.

Enlisted in 23rd Royal Fusiliers (1st Sportsmans') in October 1914. Served in France from November 1915, and was engaged at Battles of Cambrai, Festubert, &c. Discharged on 25th March 1916 as result of an accident.

LIEUT.-COLONEL MAURICE RHYND DICKSON, D.S.O., Arbroath.

Received Commission in Royal Scots Fusiliers in September 1914, and was later transferred to 12th Battalion Argyll and Sutherland Highlanders. Served in France and Macedonia, Salonica, from 1915 till 1918. Promoted to the rank of Lieut.-Colonel commanding Battalion. Awarded D.S.O. and Order of the Legion of Honour (Officier) France. Twice mentioned in Dispatches.

LIEUTENANT ALEXANDER DOUGAL, 36 Morningside Grove, Edinburgh.

Received Commission as 2nd Lieutenant in Forth Royal Garrison Artillery in November 1915. Served in France with Siege Battery as First Lieutenant from November 1917 onwards.

MAJOR WILLIAM CUNNINGHAM DUDGEON, 17 Rutland Street, Edinburgh.

Served from September 1914 to October 1918 with 2/10th Royal Scots. Thereafter in Ireland with 1/10th Royal Scots.

MAJOR ROBERT WILLIAM DUNDAS, M.C., 16 St Andrew Square, Edinburgh.

Received Commission as 2nd Lieutenant in 8th Royal Scots (T.F.) in July 1915. Was attached to Headquarters Lines of Communication, France, in November 1916. Appointed Staff Captain Headquarters Machine-Gun Corps (Heavy Branch), France, from January 1917. In June 1917 was appointed D.A.Q.M.G. Headquarters, Tank Corps, France. Promoted Temporary Major 1917. Awarded Military Cross 1918. Mentioned in Dispatches 1919.

**CAPTAIN WILLIAM HUGH ROBERTSON DURHAM,** 13 Glencairn Crescent, Edinburgh.

Received Commission as Lieutenant in 10th Battalion Scottish Rifles in August 1914. Thereafter promoted Captain. Proceeded to France and was killed in action at Loos in September 1915.

LIEUTENANT WILLIAM FAIRLEY, Troqueer, Slateford, Midlothian (Apprentice.)

Received Commission as 2nd Lieutenant Northumbrian Brigade Royal Field Artillery. Served in France from 1st July till 16th July 1916, June and July 1917, and from April 1918 onwards. Promoted Lieutenant 1st June 1916. Wounded in July 1917 at Heninel near Arras.

MAJOR JOHN IRELAND FALCONER, 71 Hanover Street, Edinburgh. (Apprentice.)

Received Commission as Lieutenant in 9th Royal Scots on 1st October 1914. Promoted Captain and Adjutant 4th March 1915; Major 5th July 1916. Served in England and Ireland 1914-18, and in France 1918-19.

CAPTAIN FRANCIS HAMILTON FASSON, 10 Murrayfield Drive, Edinburgh.

Received Commission in Scottish Horse in August 1914. Served in Gallipoli, Egypt, and Salonica. Captain and Adjutant 2nd Scottish Horse. Seconded to Remount Services Salonica 1918. Twice mentioned in Dispatches.

JAMES SOMERLED FORSYTH, Isle of Mull.

Enlisted in 63rd Canadians in August 1915. Served in France from August till November 1916. Taken prisoner, and was eighteen months in Germany and Switzerland. Repatriated to England in June 1918, and discharged in Canada in December 1918 as unfit for further service, owing to wounds received at Battle of the Somme.

**CAPTAIN ROWLAND FRASER,** Invermay, Perth. (Apprentice.)

Gazetted 2nd Lieutenant 1st Rifle Brigade on 15th August 1914. Served in this country and proceeded to France 4th January 1915. Promoted Lieutenant and thereafter Captain. Killed in action 1st July 1916.

**LIEUTENANT IAN GALLETLY,** Inchdrewer, Colinton, Midlothian. (Apprentice.)

Received Commission as 2nd Lieutenant Lowland Brigade Royal Field Artillery August 1914. Latterly attached to the Highland Division. Promoted Lieutenant. Trained in this country until October 1915. Served in France from that date until August 1916. Killed in action at Mametz Wood near Albert on 3rd August 1916.

LIEUTENANT ARTHUR WILLIAM GARDEN, Uttershill, Penicuik, Midlothian.

Gazetted Second Lieutenant in Royal Army Service Corps in September 1914. Promoted Lieutenant March 1915. Served at home and with Salonica Field Force from September 1914 to March 1919.

JOHN GAVIN (JUN.), 15 Royal Terrace, Edinburgh. (Apprentice.)

Enlisted 2nd December 1915 in 9th Royal Scots. Thereafter transferred to 469th Home Service Employment Company. Promoted Acting Sergeant. Engaged in recruiting work in this country.

2ND LIEUTENANT ROBERT GIBB, 25 East Claremont Street, Edinburgh.

Joined Royal Field Artillery as Gunner 5th August 1917. Thereafter 2nd Lieutenant Royal Army Service Corps.

CAPTAIN JAMES GILL, 26 Rutland Street, Edinburgh. (Apprentice.)

Joined Royal Garrison Artillery as a Gunner February 1916. Served in this country until April 1917; thereafter in France until February 1919. Promoted during service to rank of Acting Captain.

LIEUTENANT CHARLES AUGUSTINE GORDON, Drimnin, Argyllshire.

Enlisted in 8th Royal Scots in February 1915. Received Commission in 9th Royal Scots in July 1915. Attached to Labour Corps in August, and served in France and Belgium from September 1916 to November 1919. Wounded in August 1917.

LIEUTENANT WILLIAM JOHN GORDON, Windhouse, Mid Yell, Shetland.

Joined Royal Naval Volunteer Reserve in January 1915. Served as Officer Commanding Royal Naval Reserve Patrols and Guns Crew in Islands of Yell and Fetlar.

LIEUTENANT CHARLES LINDESAY PLAYFAIR GRACE, St Andrews.

Joined Highland Cyclist Battalion February 1915. Served on Coast Defence in Scotland until April 1918 and thereafter in Ireland.

CAPTAIN ANGUS MACLAINE GREGORSON, Ardtornish, Colinton.

Commissioned 9th Royal Scots 1st October 1914. Served on Army Recruiting Staff, Ministry of National Service, and 4th Reserve Battalion Royal Scots.

MAJOR HENRY JAMES GRIERSON, Laguna, Murthly, Perthshire.

Received Commission in Royal Highlanders (Black Watch) in October 1914. Acted as Commandant for School of Instruction for N.C.O.'s from October till November 1916. Served in France on Special Duty November 1916. A.P.M., No. 12 Area, Dover Garrison, January 31st 1917 to November 17th 1919.

**2nd LIEUTENANT JAMES GILBERT HAMILTON-GRIERSON,** 7 Palmerston Place, Edinburgh.

Enlisted in 4th Royal Scots in August 1914. Received Commission as 2nd Lieutenant Royal Scots Fusiliers on 23rd October 1914. Landed at Gallipoli in May 1915, and was killed in action near Cape Helles on 12th July 1915.

MAJOR JOHN GRIEVE, 8 Midmar Gardens, Edinburgh.

Mobilised in August 1914. Promoted Lieutenant and served in 52nd (Lowland) Divisional Train (Army Service Corps) and 10th (Irish) Divisional Army Service Corps. Served in Egypt from June till October 1915; Serbia from October till December 1915; Macedonia from December 1915 till September 1917; and in Palestine from September 1917 till May 1918. Promoted Major. Mentioned in Dispatches.

CAPTAIN WILLIAM JOHN GUILD, 5 Royal Circus, Edinburgh.

Received Commission as 2nd Lieutenant Royal Field Artillery in February 1915. Attached to 48th Divisional Artillery, and with 35th Divisional Artillery served in France from August 1915 till September 1915, and from January till September 1916. Appointed Acting Captain.

LIEUTENANT CHARLES GUTHRIE, 1 North Charlotte Street, Edinburgh.

Served with Royal Flying Corps and Royal Air Force as Squadron Equipment Officer of 76 Squadron. Engaged in defence of Hull and district. Thereafter as Wing Equipment Officer of 49th Wing engaged in Inner Defence of London (both of 6th Brigade Royal Air Force).

2ND LIEUTENANT ALEXANDER HARPER, 139 Warrender Park Road, Edinburgh.

Enlisted in Argyll and Sutherland Highlanders in May 1915. Served in France from June 1916 till March 1918, and fought at Beaumont Hamel, Arras, and Bourlon Wood. Received a Commission in Royal Scots. Returned to this country March 1918.

CAPTAIN GEORGE FRANCIS HENDERSON, M.C., 31 Charlotte Square, Edinburgh.

Received Commission as 2nd Lieutenant 3rd Scottish Horse in August 1914. Attached in October 1916 to 10th (Lovat Scouts) Battalion Cameron Highlanders. Served in Gallipoli from August 1915 till November 1915; Egypt from January till October 1916; Salonica from October 1916 till June 1918; and in France from June till December 1918. Promoted Captain 1916. Awarded Military Cross.

LIEUTENANT GILBERT LINDSAY DOUGLAS HOLE, 31 Melville Street, Edinburgh.

Enlisted 25th May 1916 in 10th K.L.R. Liverpool Scottish. Received Commission 15th January 1917. Served in France July 1917 to February 1918, when sent home with diseased eye. Served in Belgium from date of Armistice until demoblised in February 1919.

CAPTAIN ARTHUR HENRY CECIL HOPE, 57 Great King Street, Edinburgh. (Apprentice.)

Gazetted 2nd Lieutenant in 4th Seaforth Highlanders. Attached to Headquarters Indian (afterwards XVII.) Corps and thereafter to Royal Field Corps. Served in this country and in France. Mentioned in Dispatches.

CAPTAIN JAMES NAPIER HOTCHKIS, St Andrews.

Mobilised with Highland Cyclist Battalion in August 1914. Transferred to Royal Field Artillery in January 1915, and to Highland Light Infantry July 1916. Served in France and Belgium from July 1915 till January 1916, and at Malta from November 1917 to November 1919.

CAPTAIN EVAN AUSTIN HUNTER, O.B.E., 7 York Place, Edinburgh.

Received Commission as 2nd Lieutenant Army Service Corps Scottish Horse Mounted Brigade (T.F.) September 1914. Went to France in March 1917 and was invalided home. Appointed Staff Captain War Office in December 1917, and held that position till March 1919. Awarded O.B.E. Mentioned in Dispatches.

LIEUTENANT THOMAS JAMES GIBSON HUNTER, 34 St Andrew Square, Edinburgh.

Enlisted in 7th Argyll and Sutherland Highlanders in June 1916. Received Commission as 2nd Lieutenant in September 1917 and posted to Labour Corps. Promoted Lieutenant. Served in France for twenty-two months.

MAJOR JOSEPH ELLIS INGLIS, M.C., 86 Great King Street, Edinburgh.

Mobilised as Lieutenant in Royal Garrison Artillery in August 1914. Served in this country for eighteen months and thereafter in France. Attached to the Artillery Staff. Promoted Major. Awarded Military Cross and mentioned in Dispatches.

LIEUTENANT RICHARD MORISON IRELAND, 26 St Albans Road, Edinburgh.

Received Commission as 2nd Lieutenant 5th Royal Scots in September 1914. Promoted Temporary Captain October 1916. Served in Gallipoli with 5th Royal Scots and 1st Essex Regiment from September to December 1915, and in France with 9th Royal Scots from August 1916 till February 1917. Thereafter as Branch Intelligence Officer IV. Corps until demobilised in April 1919. Invalided from Gallipoli December 1915, and wounded at Beaumont Hamel in November 1916.

2ND LIEUTENANT JAMES GORDON JACK, 12 Duke Street, Edinburgh.

Enlisted as Gunner in Forth Garrison Artillery in November 1915. Obtained Commission as 2nd Lieutenant in 1st (R) Garrison Battalion Highland Light Infantry. Served in France with 4th Labour Company from June 1917 till January 1918. Invalided June 1918.

MAJOR GEORGE ERSKINE JACKSON, M.C., 26 Rutland Square, Edinburgh.

Mobilised as Staff Captain Highland Mounted Brigade in August 1914. Served in Gallipoli from September 1915 till December 1915; appointed D.A.A. & Q.M.G. Western Force. Appointed to Egyptian Expeditionary Force in June 1916. In July 1917 appointed D.A.A.G. Australian Division and served in all operations of E.E.F., including capture of Beersheba and Jerusalem in 1917, and capture of Damascus and Aleppo in 1918. Promoted Major. Awarded Military Cross and mentioned in Dispatches.

LIEUTENANT ANDREW ST CLAIR JAMESON, 16 Coates Crescent, Edinburgh. (Apprentice.)

Enlisted October 1914 in Inns of Court O.T.C. Gazetted 2nd Lieutenant 3rd Battalion Seaforth Highlanders; thereafter Lieutenant. Served in this country from October 1914 to April 1915, and in France from April 1915 to July 1916. Served in operations in second Battle of Ypres and first Battle of Somme. Wounded 1st July 1916 in the attack on Beaumont Hamel.

LIEUTENANT HARRY AULDJO JAMIESON, 66 Queen Street, Edinburgh.

Received Commission as 2nd Lieutenant 2/8th Battalion Royal Scots in January 1915. Seconded for service with Machine-Gun Corps in July 1916. Promoted Lieutenant June 1916; later appointed Acting Captain and thereafter Acting Major. Served in this country until March 1917. From then until March 1919 served in Palestine. Took part in operations at Gaza and Jerusalem.

STAFF CAPTAIN CHARLES GRAY KENNAWAY, Kenwood Park, Auchterarder. (Apprentice.)

Enlisted 4th August 1914 in 6th Battalion Royal Highlanders (Black Watch). Transferred to 1st Battalion Grenadier Guards. Promoted Staff Captain. Served in this country and in France until August 1919. Wounded 10th October 1917.

LIEUTENANT ALLAN EBENEZER KER, V.C., The Gordon Highlanders.

Received Commission as 2nd Lieutenant in the Gordon Highlanders 11th June 1915. France October 1915. Seconded for duty with Machine-Gun Corps March 1916. Embarked for Salonica July 1916. Present at battle of Macukovo, &c., near the river Vardar. Invalided with Malignant Malaria and arrived home December 1916. Promoted Lieutenant 1st January 1917. France, May 1917 to March 1918. Took part in fighting at Arras, Ypres, Cambrai, and St Quentin. Taken prisoner at St Quentin 21st March 1918. Prisoner of war at Karlsruhe March to July 1918, and at Beeskow in der Mark July to December 1918. Secretary and Food Controller, for British officers at both those Lagers. Awarded V.C. for most conspicuous bravery and devotion to duty at St Quentin on 21st March 1918.

**CAPTAIN JOHN COLLIE KINMONT,** Grange Neuk, Fountainhall Road, Edinburgh. (Apprentice.)

After serving in Officers' Training Corps, obtained Commission in 1st Battalion Queen's Own Cameron Highlanders in February 1914, but transferred to 3rd Reserve Battalion in the following May to enable him to commence his apprenticeship. Went to France with 1st Battalion in January 1915 and took part in the fighting at Cuinchy, Givenchy, Bethune, and La Basse. Contracted frostbite and was wounded and was invalided home. Was Adjutant of the Edinburgh School of Musketry for two months. Served for two years on the Staff in Edinburgh as A.D.C. to G.O.C. Scottish Coast Defence, and in March 1917 was attached to Tank Corps and returned to France as Second in Command of a Detachment. Took part in the operations on the Western Front, and was killed near Gouzecourt, Etricourt, in front of Cambrai, in November 1917. Held the rank of Captain.

LIEUTENANT GEORGE WILLIAM BALFOUR-KINNEAR, 35 Queen Street, Edinburgh.

Enlisted 15th March 1915 37th Battalion Canadian Expeditionary Force. Crossed to England in June 1916. Served as Signalling Instructor and was discharged 29th August 1917 as medically unfit.

LIEUTENANT GEORGE PURVES-RUSSELL BALFOUR-KINNEAR, 35 Queen Street, Edinburgh.

Received Commission in Royal Flying Corps in May 1916. Went to France in June 1916 as Equipment Officer. Took part in 1st Battle of the Somme and was invalided home in December 1916. Afterwards gazetted to the Staff of the Air Ministry, London. Mentioned in Dispatches.

GEORGE MURRAY LAWSON, 13 Melville Street, Edinburgh.

Enlisted in Royal Fusiliers in August 1916. Served in France from November 1916 till April 1917 when wounded and returned to this country. Relegated to Army Reserve in January 1918.

CAPTAIN JAMES G. GREENSHIELDS LEADBETTER, M.C., Younger of Spital Tower, Denholm, Roxburghshire. (Apprentice.)

Received Commission as 2nd Lieutenant in 1st Lanarkshire Yeomanry 21st January 1914. Promoted Lieutenant 28th October 1915 and Captain 27th June 1917. Served in Gallipoli from 27th September 1915 until 31st December 1915. Thereafter in Egypt, Palestine, and Syria until 27th January 1919. Awarded Military Cross.

LIEUT.-COLONEL ARCHIBALD STEWART LESLIE, C.M.G., T.D., 33 Queen Street, Edinburgh.

Mobilised with 1st Scottish Horse as Major in August 1914. Served at Dardanelles from August 1915 till September 1915, when invalided home. Attached to War Office Staff from September 1916 till April 1917; appointed Directorate of Forestry, France, in April 1917. Promoted Lieut.-Colonel. Awarded C.M.G. and mentioned in Dispatches.

**CAPTAIN WILLIAM LIDDLE,** 5 Hill Street, Edinburgh.

Received Commission as 2nd Lieutenant in 9th Royal Scots. Thereafter promoted Captain. Served in France and Flanders. Died from double pneumonia on 27th September 1918 at Casualty Clearing Station.

CAPTAIN ROBERT STRATHERN LINDSAY, M.C., 49 Manor Place, Edinburgh. (Apprentice.)

Gazetted 2nd Lieutenant 9th Battalion the Royal Scots. Promoted Lieutenant and thereafter Captain. Served in this country from 4th August 1914 until 23rd February 1915, and in France from 23rd February 1915 until 30th March 1919. Awarded Military Cross January 1917.

GEORGE LORIMER, 22 Rutland Square, Edinburgh.

Enlisted in Royal Garrison Artillery in September 1916. After ten months on Coast Defence went to France and served there and in Belgium for eighteen months.

**CAPTAIN JAMES BANNERMAN LORIMER**, 9 Gloucester Place, Edinburgh.

Enlisted in 9th Royal Scots in August 1914. Promoted Lieutenant 8th Cameron Highlanders in December 1914. Received Captaincy February 1916. Served in this country from August 1914 until August 1916. Went to France attached to 5th Cameron Highlanders. Posted missing. Presumed killed at Battle of Rœux near Arras on 3rd May 1917.

LIEUTENANT JOHN DONALDSON LOWNIE, 7 Admiral Terrace, Edinburgh.

Received Commission as 2nd Lieutenant the Royal Scots in July 1915. Seconded to Machine-Gun Corps October 1916. Served in France from February till June 1917. Wounded while serving with the Machine-Gun Corps at Messines Ridge. Served at home from June 1917 onwards. Promoted 1st Lieutenant February 1917.

LIEUTENANT JOHN HUGH LOWSON, 9 Great Stuart Street, Edinburgh.

Received Commission 25th August 1914 12th Royal Scots. Served in that Battalion in France. Appointed Divisional Instructor Bombs and Gas for 9th Division. Transferred to R.F.C. 26th August 1916. Wounded and captured 27th September 1916. Repatriated 28th December 1918.

LIEUT.-COLONEL DAVID LYELL, V.D., 39 Castle Street, Edinburgh.

Appointed Secretary of Midlothian, Linlithgow, and Peebles Territorial Force Associations 14th January 1915. Relieved of his duties 30th June 1919. Twice mentioned in Dispatches.

LIEUTENANT ALFRED CHARLES MACAULAY, 13 Melville Street, Edinburgh. (Apprentice.)

Enlisted in Royal Air Force 24th September 1917. Received Commission 7th February 1918. Joined 43rd Squadron as Flying Officer and served in France until 4th August 1918. Demobilised 5th February 1919.

MAJOR JAMES HAROLD MACDONALD, T.D., 19 York Place, Edinburgh.

Gazetted Captain 7th Royal Scots September 1914. Promoted Major June 1916. Served in France with 9th Royal Scots in 1917 and was wounded. Attached Headquarters, Tay Defences, June 1918.

CAPTAIN ROBERT McCOSH, O.B.E., M.C., Southernwood, Davidson's Mains.

Received Commission as 2nd Lieutenant Lanarkshire Yeomanry in September 1914. Service in Gallipoli, Egypt, and Palestine from 1915-19. Promoted Staff Captain 1917, D.A.Q.M.G. 1918. Awarded O.B.E. (Military), and Military Cross, and Order of the Nile. Mentioned in Dispatches.

**2nd LIEUTENANT DAVID CAMPBELL MACEWEN,** 9 Douglas Crescent, Edinburgh.

Received Commission in Royal Scots in December 1915. Proceeded to France in August 1916 and took part in the operations on the Somme. Towards the end of that year went through the successful action at Beaumont Hamel. Subsequently saw service in other parts of the line. Whilst leading his platoon against the German trenches in the attack on Vimy Ridge at the opening of the Battle of Arras on 9th April 1917, seriously wounded, and died at a Casualty Clearing Station on 10th April 1917. Buried in Military Cemetery, Aubigny.

LIEUTENANT JEFFREY BLACKSTOCK M'GLASHAN, Gatehouse-on-Fleet.

Enlisted in 9th Royal Scots 1st September 1914. Received Commission as 2nd Lieutenant in 6th Argyll and Sutherland Highlanders 15th January 1915. Promoted Lieutenant 1st June 1916. Served in Belgium from January 1917 to August 1917, and in France and Italy from August 1917 to November 1918. Gassed while with 51st Division near Maing (Valenciennes Area) 25th October 1918. Served with 3rd Argyll and Sutherland Highlanders in Ireland and Scotland until 15th July 1919.

LIEUTENANT AUGUSTUS WALLACE MACGREGOR, Northern Club, George Street, Edinburgh.

Received Commission as 2nd Lieutenant in 4th K.O.S.B. 19th November 1915. Served at various stations in this country. Promoted Lieutenant 1st July 1917.

CAPTAIN DUNCAN GERALD M'GREGOR, 27 Royal Terrace, Edinburgh. (Apprentice.)

Received Commission as Sub-Lieutenant R.N.V.R. 14th June 1916. Captain Royal Air Force. Seaplane Observer in North Sea Anti-Submarine patrol from March 1917 to Armistice. Mentioned in Dispatches April 1918, and awarded the Air Force Cross 4th November 1918.

CAPTAIN JOHN GEORGE HUNTER M'INTOSH, 15 Young Street, Edinburgh.

Served with Scottish Horse and Lovat Scouts. In this country until August 1915. Thereafter in Gallipoli, Egypt, and Salonica. In France from June 1918 until signing of Armistice.

LIEUTENANT JAMES WATSON M'ISAAC, Royal Bank House, Elgin.

Enlisted in Gordon Highlanders. Received a Commission as Lieutenant in Highland Light Infantry and served with the Salonica Forces.

**CAPTAIN WILLIAM ROBERT BENNY McJANNET.**

Enlisted November 1914 in 10th Seaforth Highlanders. Received Commission as Captain in January 1915. Served in various training camps in this country until 8th June 1916. Thereafter served in France with 7th Seaforth Highlanders. Killed in action 15th July 1916.

LIEUT.-COLONEL JAMES FRANCIS MACKAY, Whitehouse, Cramond.

1st October 1914 to 11th August 1915 Assistant Recruiting Officer, Recruiting Staff Office, Edinburgh. 11th August 1915 to July 1917 O.C. Administrative Centre, Lowland City of Edinburgh Royal Garrison Artillery, and 138 Territorial Force Depot Edinburgh (No. 2). August 1917 to 31st December 1918 Military Representative to the City of Edinburgh Tribunal.

CAPTAIN DAVID MACKENZIE, 1 Atholl Place, Edinburgh.

Received Commission as 2nd Lieutenant 2/6th Royal Highlanders (Black Watch) October 1914. Served in Mesopotamia during 1917-18 and was attached to 4th Hants Regiment. Promoted Captain.

LIEUTENANT JAMES MOIR MACKENZIE, 26 Kingsburgh Road, Edinburgh.

Received Commission as Temporary Sub-Lieutenant R.N.V.R. in October 1914. Was Adjutant of the 4th Batt. R.N.D., Crystal Palace, from October 1914 till April 1916. Granted permanent Commission R.N.V.R. From April 1916 till January 1919 served as Assistant Gunnery Officer and Watchkeeper on H.M.S. "Loyal" (1916-17), H.M.S. "Tempest" (1917-18), and H.M.S. "Shakespeare" (1918-19). Promoted Lieutenant.

**CAPTAIN KENNETH MACKENZIE** of Dolphinton, and 20 Ainslie Place, Edinburgh.

Received Commission as Lieutenant 2/9th Royal Scots October 1914. Promoted Captain 1915. Afterwards attached to 7th Royal Scots. When stationed at Leith Docks received Medal for saving, at great personal risk, a man who had fallen in. Went to France in March 1918 and was killed in action between Heninel and Fontaine les Croisilles on 27th August 1918.

**CAPTAIN JOHN MACKINTOSH,** Bank House, Hopeman, Morayshire. (Apprentice.)

Received Commission as 2nd Lieutenant 6th Seaforth Highlanders in September 1914. Latterly Captain. Trained recruits in this country until June 1917. Thereafter went to France. Was wounded in November 1917 at Flesquieres, whence sent to England. Returned to France in April 1918, and was killed on 23rd July of that year at St Imoges on the Rheims. Twice mentioned in Dispatches.

CAPTAIN CHARLES FELLOWES MONCRIEFFE MACLACHLAN, 71 George Street, Edinburgh.

Enlisted in 16th Royal Scots December 1914. Obtained Commission as 2nd Lieutenant in 11th Gordon Highlanders March 1915. Posted 9th Gordon Highlanders, B.E.F., October 1915. Served in France from October 1915 to March 1918. Adjutant August 1916 to March 1918. Attached 1/1 Highland Cyclist Battalion April 1918. In Ireland April 1918 to March 1919. Acting Adjutant. 1914-15 Star. Mentioned in Dispatches.

LIEUTENANT DUNCAN MACNAUGHTON, Dundurawe, Arboretum Road, Edinburgh.

Mobilised as Private with 9th Royal Scots in August 1914. Received Commission as Lieutenant 3rd Gordon Highlanders in January 1915. Went to Belgium (Ypres Section) in March 1915 and was wounded in August of that year, and returned to this country. Was placed on retired list in January 1917 in consequence of wounds.

**LIEUTENANT PETER JOHN STEWART MACPHAIL,** 7 Craigmillar Park, Edinburgh.

Joined O.T.C. in September 1915, and after training obtained Commission as 2nd Lieutenant in Royal Garrison Artillery. Went to France in January 1917. Was slightly wounded in March 1918 and afterwards suffered from shell-shock. In May 1918 found unfit for general service and returned to this country. In November 1918 contracted pneumonia and died on 26th of that month at Magdalene Camp Hospital, Winchester. Prior to death promoted Lieutenant. Served as Temporary Adjutant.

**CAPTAIN ALEXANDER WILLIAM URQUHART MACRAE,** 14 Gloucester Place, Edinburgh.

Mobilised with 5th Royal Scots in August 1914, and went to Gallipoli with 29th Division in April 1915. Took part in many engagements, and was wounded in the head at Fir Tree Wood when making an attack against the Turks. Again severely wounded, and on recovering was sent first to Egypt and then to France. Afterwards wounded twice, and appointed Second in Command of the 52nd Batt. Devonshire Regiment at home. Returned to France and fell in action on 11th August 1918, at Parvilliers, while leading his men.

LIEUTENANT CHRISTOPHER R. M'VITTIE, 15 Rutland Street, Edinburgh. (Apprentice.)

Mobilised as Sergeant in 4th Battalion the Royal Scots. Promoted C.Q.M.S. March 1915. Landed at Gallipoli 14th June 1915. Wounded 12th July 1915. Promoted C.S.M. August 1915. Returned to Gallipoli and took part in evacuation of Cape Helles January 1916. Promoted 2nd Lieutenant and attached to 12th Royal Scots. Served in France January to April 1917. Promoted Lieutenant April 1918. Discharged on account of wounds received in France.

CAPTAIN GILBERT CUMMING MANFORD, M.C., 25 Mayfield Road, Edinburgh.

Received Commission as 2nd Lieutenant 14th Highland Light Infantry in November 1914. Served in France from June 1916 till 1918. Promoted Captain and Adjutant June 1916. Awarded Military Cross. Demobilised May 1919.

LIEUTENANT TERTIUS PETER MANUEL, Duncruin, Comiston Road, Edinburgh.

Received Commission as 2nd Lieutenant in July 1915 in 6th Royal Scots. Attached Machine-Gun Corps. Served abroad from March till August 1917, and served in this country from that date. Promoted Lieutenant February 1917.

2ND LIEUTENANT ROBERT WADDELL MARSHALL, 5 Thistle Street, Edinburgh. (Apprentice.)

Enlisted in Argyll and Sutherland Highlanders May 1916. Gazetted 2nd Lieutenant 16th Battalion the Rifle Brigade 29th August 1917. Served in France from 9th November 1917 until 31st January 1919.

2ND LIEUTENANT ROBERT WATSON MARTIN, 32 Charlotte Square, Edinburgh. (Apprentice.)

Joined Royal Flying Corps as Cadet 13th April 1917. Enlisted in London Scottish 13th October 1917. Gazetted 2nd Lieutenant in Royal Highlanders (Black Watch) 31st July 1918. Served in this country.

**CAPTAIN (ACTING MAJOR) JAMES DOUGLAS LEITCH MELROSE**, Goshen Bank, Kelso.

Mobilised with Royal Garrison Artillery (T.F.) as Lieutenant in 1914. Went to France in August 1916, and died in France from wounds received in action on 25th April 1918. Promoted Captain and acted as Major.

LIEUTENANT PATRICK DROUGHT NORTH MENZIES, Canaan House, Edinburgh.

Joined Edinburgh University O.T.C. in March 1916. From August till November 1916 Private in Oxford and Bucks Light Infantry 6th Cadet Battalion, Worcester College, Oxford. From January 1917 to November 1918 served in Fife and Forfar Yeomanry. Obtained a Commission and went to France in November 1918, and was attached to 5th Royal Scots Fusiliers.

CAPTAIN JOHN SYDNEY LAWRENCE MILLAR, 27 Ann Street, Edinburgh.

Mobilised 5th August 1914 as Lieutenant 2nd Lovat Scouts; afterwards attached to Royal Engineers Signal Service. Went to Gallipoli in September 1915. Served as Signalling Officer with Egyptian Expeditionary Force first as O.C. Signals, Kharga Column, Western Force, and latterly in Palestine with the Signal Squadron, Australian Mounted Division, till September 1918. Present at capture of Beersheba and Jerusalem. Thereafter O.C. Signals, Midland District, Ireland, till May 1919. Promoted Captain 1917.

CAPTAIN ALEXANDER GRANT SCHAW MILLAR, 11 Douglas Crescent, Edinburgh. (Apprentice.)

Served as Cadet with 1/1st Fife and Forfar Yeomanry from 29th September 1914 to 28th October 1914, when Gazetted 2nd Lieutenant 2/1st Fife and Forfar Yeomanry. Attached 2/1st Highland Mounted Brigade H.I. for staff duties. Lieutenant 1st June 1916. Adjutant 2/1st Fife and Forfar Yeomanry 8th September 1916 to 13th March 1919. Gazetted Captain 25th January 1918. Mentioned in War Office List of Mentions (Irish Command).

ALFRED ERNEST MILNE, 40 Coates Gardens, Edinburgh.

Enlisted as Private in 4th Royal Scots in July 1916, and was afterwards transferred to 10th Royal Scots. Went to Russia in September 1918 and was wounded in October 1918.

**LIEUTENANT-COLONEL JAMES THOMSON RANKIN MITCHELL, D.S.O.,** Bannockburn House, Bannockburn.

Mobilised in 11th Argyll and Sutherland Highlanders as 2nd Lieutenant. Went to France as Captain in June 1915; Second in Command of 13th Royal Scots. Wounded before Arras on 28th March 1918, and died from wounds in Queen Alexandra Hospital, London, on 1st April 1918 Promoted Lieut.-Colonel. Awarded D.S.O. and Croix de Guerre (France). Several times mentioned in Dispatches.

CAPTAIN JOHN STUART MORTON, 20 Queen Street, Edinburgh.

Received Commission as 2nd Lieutenant 2nd Battalion Royal Scots 2nd May 1917. Promoted Captain April 1918. Relinquished Commission October 1918 and enlisted as Private in 28th Battalion London Regiment (Artists' Rifles). Transferred to Inns of Court O.T.C. 30th December 1918.

CAPTAIN GAVIN BLACK LOUDON MOTHERWELL, O.B.E., 42 York Place, Edinburgh.

Received Commission as 2nd Lieutenant 2/4th Royal Scots Fusiliers in October 1914. Thereafter promoted Captain. From March 1916 acted as Appeal Military Representative to Appeal Tribunals for the Counties of Stirling, Dumbarton, and Clackmannan, and also for Argyllshire. Awarded O.B.E. (Military Division).

CAPTAIN KENNETH MURRAY, 9 Buckingham Terrace, Edinburgh.

Mobilised in August 1914 with 2nd Lovat Scouts Yeomanry as 2nd Lieutenant. Served in Gallipoli from September to December 1915, in Egypt from January till August 1916, and in Salonica from September 1916 till January 1917. Promoted Captain. Discharged in November 1918 on account of ill-health caused by wounds received at Salonica.

CAPTAIN ALEXANDER LOW MUSTARD, 1 North Street, Elgin.

Mobilised in August 1914 with 6th Royal Scots as Lieutenant. Served in France with 15th Royal Scots and 34th Divisional Depot Battalion from February 1917; was wounded on 12th April 1918, and returned to this country. Served as Assistant Instructor at Officers' Convalescent Hospitals and Command Depots from July 1918. Promoted Captain.

**LIEUTENANT JAMES GRAHAM MYLNE,** 10 Ainslie Place, Edinburgh.

Received Commission as 2nd Lieutenant in 2/8th Royal Scots. Afterwards attached to 1/4th Royal Scots. Promoted 1st Lieutenant. Served in Palestine, and thereafter in France. Killed in action 2nd September 1918.

MAJOR ARCHIBALD DAVID MUTTER NAPIER, 22 Clarendon Crescent, Edinburgh.

Commissioned as Captain of 17th Northumberland Fusiliers in November 1914. Transferred to 21st Northumberland Fusiliers February 1915. Went to France in January 1916 and took part in hostilities at Armentières, Somme, and Vimy Ridge. Promoted Major on the field in July 1916. Invalided April 1917. Mentioned in Dispatches.

LIEUTENANT HAROLD STANLEY NICOLSON. (Apprentice.)

Joined R.N.V.R. January 1915. Served on Board H.M.S. "Resolution."

FLIGHT CADET JOHN PATRICK PATTULLO, 16 Grosvenor Street, Edinburgh. (Apprentice.)

Enlisted in Royal Air Force as Air Mechanic 3rd May 1918. Served in France for four months. Demobilised 24th February 1919.

LIEUTENANT ROBERT OCTAVIUS PITMAN, 48 Castle Street, Edinburgh.

Received Commission as 2nd Lieutenant 11th Hussars in September 1916. Served in France from October 1916 till December 1918.

CAPTAIN WILLIAM MISKIN POTTER, 4 Gillsland Road, Edinburgh. (Apprentice.)

Enlisted 1st October 1914. Attached to 10th Seaforth Highlanders and thereafter 8th Service Battalion Seaforth Highlanders. Promoted Captain. Served at home and in France. Wounded and gassed 13th October 1916.

CAPTAIN NORMAN SETH PRINGLE-PATTISON, 57 Castle Street, Edinburgh.

Received Commission as 2nd Lieutenant 7th Royal Scots in September 1914. Served in Gallipoli from August till November 1915, when invalided home. Went to France to 9th Royal Scots in May 1917 and took part in the Battles of Ypres (1917), Cambrai, and St Quentin. Was wounded in March 1918 and returned to this country. Promoted Captain.

CAPTAIN NEIL GODFREY PAULIN, 6 Forres Street, Edinburgh. (Apprentice.)

Mobilised as Lieutenant 1st Lowland Brigade R.F.A. (T.), August 1914. Served in France from October 1915 to February 1917, and with 86th Army F.A. Brigade from February 1917 to May 1919. Promoted Captain. Wounded in third Battle of Ypres June 1917.

**LIEUTENANT JOHN PROSSER, Jun.,** 19 York Place, Edinburgh.

Received Commission as 2nd Lieutenant 2/4th Royal Highlanders (Black Watch) December 1914. Adjutant with rank of Acting Captain 1916-17. In July 1918 went to France as Lieutenant and was attached to 8th Royal Highlanders (Black Watch). Was killed on 28th September 1918 while taking part in the advance of the British Second Army in concert with the Belgian Army in Flanders.

**2nd LIEUTENANT JAMES PHILIP PURVES,** Uganda.

Joined Oxford University Cadet Corps in June 1916 and received Commission as 2nd Lieutenant in the 6th Argyll and Sutherland Highlanders in October 1916, and was latterly attached to the 7th Argyll and Sutherland Highlanders. Went to France in January 1917, and was killed in the neighbourhood of Bethune on 11th April 1918 whilst leading his men against the Germans in the Spring Offensive.

LIEUTENANT WILLIAM ROLAND RAINNIE, 3 Carlton Street, Edinburgh.

Received Commission as 2nd Lieutenant Royal Engineers (Signals) in February 1915. Went to France in January 1918 and was attached to 5th Army Signalling Company, and to G.H.Q. Signalling Company until July 1918.

MAJOR THOMAS RANKEN, T.D., 7 Albyn Place, Edinburgh.

Rejoined 8th Royal Scots from T.F. Reserve on 5th August 1915. Acted as Musketry Officer from February to April 1915, and as Brigade Major from April to June 1915 to 2/1 Lothian Infantry Brigade. Thereafter attached to General Staff, Scottish and Northern Commands, until 25th February 1919.

MAJOR WILLIAM BLACK RANKIN, 3 Coates Crescent, Edinburgh.

Major in 4th Highland Light Infantry, Special Reserve, which he joined in 1900, and was mobilised in August 1914. In November 1915 attached to 1st Garrison Battalion Royal Scots Fusiliers, and in January 1916 went to India. Returned to this country on sick leave and attached to 1st Garrison Battalion Highland Light Infantry until December 1918.

CAPTAIN JOHN RICHARDSON, 9 South Charlotte Street, Edinburgh. (Apprentice.)

Received Commission in 8th Royal Scots in November 1914. Served in this country and in France. Wounded August 1916. Rejoined in May 1917. Again wounded in April 1918.

CAPTAIN CHARLES RONALD RITCHIE, 20 Hill Street, Edinburgh.

Received Commission as 2nd Lieutenant Lowland Mounted Brigade Royal Army Service Corps on 25th September 1914, and served in this country until 5th May 1917. Promoted Captain 26th June 1915, and served abroad with the British Salonica Force until 5th May 1919. Twice mentioned in Dispatches, and awarded Greek Order of the Redeemer and Greek Medal of Military Merit.

**LIEUTENANT MATTHEW FREER RODGER**, Rossland, Helensburgh.

Received Commission as 2nd Lieutenant 3rd Scottish Rifles September 1914. Transferred 4th Scottish Rifles 1915 and attached 2nd Scottish Rifles in France. Promoted Lieutenant. Served in France from May 1915 to October 1916. Killed in action at Battle of the Somme on 23rd October 1916.

CAPTAIN GEORGE ARCHER RUSK, M.C. (Apprentice.)

Received Commission in 9th Royal Highlanders (Black Watch) September 1914. Served in this country until July 1915. Left for France in July. Promoted Captain. Took part in Battle of Loos September 1915. Gassed April 1916. Wounded June 1916. Thereafter attached to 3rd Black Watch at Nigg. Left for Salonica March 1917 with 10th Black Watch. Present at Battle of Varder River. Proceeded to France June 1918. With 1st Black Watch at Massigny and Mons Canal. Thereafter served in Germany and granted permanent Commission. Awarded Military Cross and mentioned in Dispatches.

**LIEUTENANT ANDREW HAMILTON SCOTT,** Dalkeith Park, Dalkeith.

Cadet Edinburgh O.T.C. from March to July 1916, when transferred to Officers' Cadet Battalion at Bristol. Received Commission as 2nd Lieutenant 4th King's Own Scottish Borderers in November 1916. Went to France and attached to 6th King's Own Scottish Borderers in January 1917, and reported missing on 3rd May 1917. Presumed killed in action.

MAJOR JOHN MENZIES BAILLIE SCOTT, Radcot, Colinton, Midlothian.

Mobilised as Lieutenant with Royal Field Artillery (T.F.) in August 1914. Promoted Captain and Adjutant in April 1915 and went to France in October 1915. Was wounded and returned to this country in October 1917. Promoted Major. Mentioned in Dispatches.

CAPTAIN AND ADJUTANT WILLIAM ISAAC HAIG-SCOTT, M.C., Cassells Place, Leith.

Received Commission as 2nd Lieutenant 4th Reserve Brigade Royal Field Artillery in September 1915. Served in France from January 1916 with Batteries, and at Headquarters 93rd Army Brigade Royal Field Artillery. Twice wounded. Awarded Military Cross and mentioned in Dispatches.

**LIEUTENANT JOHN DONALD SHAW,** 66 Haymarket Terrace, Edinburgh. (Apprentice.)

Joined 9th Royal Scots 2nd December 1915. Afterwards attached to 13th Royal Scots. Received Commission as 1st Lieutenant. Served in France until 26th July 1918, when killed in action.

CAPTAIN ALEXANDER RUSSELL SIMPSON, 10 Albyn Place, Edinburgh.

Received Commission as 2nd Lieutenant Royal Garrison Artillery on 6th October 1915. Thereafter promoted Captain. Served in Coast Defence Batteries and Commanded No. 1 Armoured Train.

LIEUTENANT SAMUEL RALEIGH SIMPSON, 10 Albyn Place, Edinburgh.

Enlisted in Army Service Corps in May 1916. Received Commission in Labour Corps in December 1917, and served in France with that Corps from February 1918.

LIEUT.-COLONEL ROBERT SIMSON, O.B.E., Colinton.

Received Commission as Captain 4th Royal Scots in September 1914. Served in Egypt from January 1916 onwards. Commandant Offices of War Camp. Commandant Officers' Base Depot, and since May 1917 Commandant Infantry Base Depot. Promoted Temporary Lieut.-Colonel. Mentioned in Dispatches. Commandant Demobilisation Camp. Awarded O.B.E. (Military).

CAPTAIN DONALD BOASE SINCLAIR, O.B.E., 43 Castle Street, Edinburgh.

Received Commission as 2nd Lieutenant 9th Royal Scots on 4th October 1914. Thereafter promoted Captain. Served as Intelligence Officer on South-East Coast of Kent. Staff Captain at War Office, and thereafter under New Recruiting Organisation.

LIEUT.-COLONEL CHILTON LIND ADDISON-SMITH, O.B.E., 3 Belgrave Crescent, Edinburgh.

Mobilised as Major and Second in Command 3rd (Reserve) Battalion Seaforth Highlanders on 5th August 1914. Promoted Temporary Lieut.-Colonel 1st December 1914. Raised and Commanded 10th (Service) Battalion Seaforth Highlanders. Served in France and Belgium with the 6th (Service) Battalion Somerset Light Infantry (1915), 27th City of Winnipeg Battalion, 6th Canadian Infantry Brigade, 2nd Division; 8th Battalion Bedfordshire Regiment, and 2nd Battalion Sherwood Foresters, 6th Division; and latterly commanded 19th Labour Group Headquarters Received O.B.E. (Military Division); mentioned in Dispatches. Order of Wen-Hu conferred by His Excellency the President of the Republic of China.

2ND LIEUTENANT GEORGE FREDERICK GRAHAM SMITH, 26 St Andrew Square, Edinburgh.

Enlisted 3rd Royal Scots Fusiliers. Promoted 2nd Lieutenant and served with 2/3rd Scottish Horse.

**2nd LIEUTENANT JOHN FRAZER SMITH,** 110 George Street, Edinburgh. (Apprentice.)

Received Commission in 7th Queen's Own Cameron Highlanders 1st August 1916. Trained in this country and went to France on 4th February 1917. Killed in action at Battle of Arras on 11th April 1917.

LIEUTENANT JOHN SMITH, 5 South Charlotte Street, Edinburgh. (Apprentice.)

Gazetted 2nd Lieutenant 5th Reserve Regiment of Cavalry 29th September 1914. Transferred to 2nd Life Guards 13th May 1915. Promoted Lieutenant. Served abroad. Mentioned in Dispatches.

LIEUTENANT RALPH COLLEY SMITH, M.C., The Firs, Selkirk.

Gazetted Lieutenant 4th Northumbrian (Howitzer) Brigade Royal Field Artillery December 1914. Promoted Acting Captain and Acting Major. Served in this country until April 1915, and in France from that date until 4th May 1917. Wounded and discharged. Awarded Military Cross.

CAPTAIN ROBERT BEVERIDGE SMITH, 24A Bernard Street, Leith.

Enlisted in Seaforth Highlanders in November 1914. Went to France in June 1916, and was severely wounded in October of that year. Promoted Captain. Mentioned in Dispatches.

CAPTAIN THOMAS STODART WHYTE SMITH, 45 Queen Street, Edinburgh.

Received Commission as 2nd Lieutenant Royal Scots in March 1915. Later Captain King's African Rifles, and served in Nyasaland and Portuguese East Africa from 1917.

LIEUTENANT PATRICK CECIL SMYTHE, O.B.E., 48 Castle Street, Edinburgh. (Apprentice.)

Received Commission as 2nd Lieutenant 6th Royal Highlanders (Black Watch) 18th January 1915. Served overseas with 6th and 9th Royal Highlanders (Black Watch) from October 1917 till April 1918. Appointed Supervisor of Physical and Recreational Training April 1918 to January 1919. Acting Captain February 1917 to July 1917. April 1918 to date of demobilisation. Awarded O.B.E. Mentioned in Dispatches.

JAMES WALKER SOMERVILLE, 76 George Street, Edinburgh.

Enlisted in 8th Battalion the Royal Scots on 1st April 1916. Thereafter transferred to 469th H.S. Employment Company (Labour Corps) and promoted Sergeant. Demobilised 28th February 1919.

CAPTAIN ROBERT SOMERVILLE, 4 Albyn Place, Edinburgh.

Joined Lowland Heavy Battery R.G.A. 4th November 1915. Thereafter served as Brigade Supply Officer, and with R.G.A. Relinquished Commission on account of ill-health on 2nd July 1918.

CAPTAIN ERIC JOHN POTT STEVENSON, Kelso. (Apprentice.)

Joined University Cadet Corps 4th August 1914. Received Commission as 2nd Lieutenant Royal Field Artillery in September 1914. Served in France and Italy from July 1915 till demobilised in April 1919. Mentioned in Dispatches from Italy.

MAJOR HENRY JAMES STEVENSON, Order of St John of Jerusalem, (T.D.), 64 Princes Street, Edinburgh.

On outbreak of war A.D.C. Headquarters 1/1 Lowland Mounted Brigade, Cupar-Fife, and thereafter appointed Brigade Major 2/1 Lowland Mounted Brigade. Served at various Headquarters in Scotland and Ireland with that Brigade as Brigade Major for three and a half years. Thereafter transferred to 4th (Reserve) Border Regiment and served in England. Twice mentioned in Dispatches and received a Brevet.

**CAPTAIN CHARLES EDWARD STEWART, M.C.**, Dunraven, Lasswade.

Enlisted in 15th Royal Scots in September 1914. Received a Commission as Lieutenant in Durham Light Infantry in November of that year. Went to France in August 1915 and took part in the fighting on the Somme. Obtained his Captaincy in September 1916. Was wounded whilst leading his Company into action at the Spring Offensive (April 1917), and died as the result of his wounds on 10th April 1917. Awarded the Military Cross, and was mentioned in Dispatches.

**LIEUTENANT JOHN JAMES ERSKINE BROWN STEWART**, 18 Royal Terrace, Edinburgh. (Apprentice.)

Received Commission as 2nd Lieutenant 8th Seaforth Highlanders in September 1914. Afterwards resigned Commission owing to defective eyesight and joined the 18th Royal Fusiliers as a private. Went to France in December 1915, and returned to this country to train for a Commission. In April 1916 received Commission as Lieutenant in 7th Royal Scots and went to France with his Company in January of the following year, being afterwards attached to the 12th Battalion Royal Scots. Died of wounds at Red Cross Hospital, Le Touquet, France, on 12th June 1917.

**LIEUTENANT JOHN WALCOT STEWART, M.C.**, 1 Rutland Square, Edinburgh.

Enlisted Lothian and Border Horse on 31st August 1914. Commissioned 1st Lieutenant 16th Royal Scots 8th April 1915. Served in this country until 7th January 1916. Proceeded to France on 8th January 1916. Wounded February 1916. Killed in action 21st March 1918. Awarded Military Cross.

CAPTAIN GEORGE SMITH GOODALL STRACHAN, 50 Queen Street, Edinburgh.

Mobilised as Lieutenant 9th Battalion The Royal Scots 4th August 1914. Served in France from 16th to 31st July 1916, and from 3rd January 1917 to 2nd May 1917. Promoted Captain. Severely wounded at Rœux on 23rd April 1917.

LIEUTENANT WILLIAM LEITCH STUART, 2 Murrayfield Gardens, Edinburgh.

Enlisted in 9th Royal Scots in August 1914, and obtained a Commission in 7th Royal Highlanders (Black Watch) in October of that year. Went to France in May 1915 and served with his Regiment until invalided home in November 1917.

CAPTAIN ROBERT TEDCASTLE, M.C., 25 Rutland Street, Edinburgh. (Apprentice.)

Enlisted in Scots Guards. Went to France in August 1916 and was wounded in the Battle of the Somme in September of that year. Received Commission in The Cheshire Regiment, and again went to France in June 1918. Wounded at Battle of the Marne in August 1918. Promoted Captain. Awarded Military Cross (action Grand-Rozoy, 28th July to 2nd August 1918).

**CAPTAIN ALAN GRAHAM THOMSON,** 11 South Charlotte Street, Edinburgh.

Received Commission as 2nd Lieutenant 7th Royal Scots in July 1915. Served in France and Belgium with 2nd Royal Scots from October 1916 till September 1917, when posted missing. Subsequently reported killed at Zonnebeke, Belgium, on 26th September 1917. Promoted Acting Captain.

LIEUTENANT FREDERICK LEWIS MAITLAND TOD, 45 Castle Street, Edinburgh.

Enlisted in 9th Royal Scots in August 1914. Afterwards obtained a Commission and served in Egypt with the Army Service Corps from June till September 1915; from October 1915 till April 1918 in Servia, Macedonia, and Palestine; and from April till September 1918 in France. Accidentally wounded on 20th September 1918.

**CAPTAIN THOMAS TODRICK,** 30 Regent Terrace, Edinburgh.

Held Captaincy in 8th Royal Scots when called up August 1914. Served in France from November to 15th December 1914. Killed in action on the latter date. Mentioned in Dispatches.

LIEUT.-COLONEL HAROLD BECKWITH TOWSE, late Royal Scots Greys, Cavalry Club, Piccadilly, London, W.

Posted to Headquarters Scottish Command as Staff Captain in August 1914. Appointed Major (2nd in command) of 25th Royal Fusiliers March 1915. Served in East Africa from March 1915 till January 1918. Posted to Staff and appointed Officer Commanding Uganda, with rank of Lieut.-Colonel, November 1915. Appointed D.A.Q.M.G., G.H.Q., France, March 1918, till demobilised July 1919. Three times mentioned in Dispatches.

MAJOR JAMES FRANCIS FRASER TYTLER, D.S.O., 1 Drumsheugh Place, Edinburgh.

Received Commission as Lieutenant in Lovat Scouts some years before the War and promoted Captain in August 1914. Afterwards attached to 10th Cameron Highlanders. Served with that Battalion in Gallipoli, Egypt, Salonica, and France. Promoted Major. Awarded D.S.O.

CAPTAIN FRANCIS WILLIAM GEORGE URQUHART, 79 Princes Street, Edinburgh.

Enlisted in Lovat Scouts in September 1914, and in the same month was granted a Commission in Army Service Corps. Went to France in November 1914 and was present with the 21st Division at Loos 1915; Arras and Ypres 1917; Kemmel Hill; Aisne-Marne Retreat, and the advance from Albert to Maubouge in 1918. Mentioned in Dispatches.

CAPTAIN HARRY WAKELIN, M.C., 137 High Street, Linlithgow.

Mobilised as Lieutenant with 10th Royal Scots in August 1914. Attached to 9th Royal Scots in April 1917. Served in France with 51st Division until 12th April 1918, when wounded at Merville. Afterwards attached to Headquarters Scottish Command. Promoted Captain. Awarded Military Cross.

CAPTAIN JAMES GLENCORSE WAKELIN, O.B.E., 14 Drummond Place, Edinburgh. (Apprentice.)

Received Commission as 2nd Lieutenant 5th Battalion Royal Scots Fusiliers. Promoted Captain. Served in Egypt, and was wounded 16th July 1915. Thereafter acted as Officer in charge of Recruiting and National Service for Ayrshire and Wigtownshire.

LIEUTENANT GEORGE WILLOUGHBY WALLACE, 7 Inverleith Row, Edinburgh.

Gazetted 2nd Lieutenant in Forth Royal Garrison Artillery (Territorial) on 14th November 1914. Promoted Lieutenant 1st June 1916, Acting Captain 1st March 1916, and Acting Major 12th September 1918. Served in this country. Demobilised 5th January 1919.

**SERGEANT JOHN DOUGLAS WATSON.**

Enlisted in September 1914 in 9th Gordon Highlanders (M.G. Section). Trained in England until 6th July 1915, then crossed to France. Killed in action, presumably at St Auguste, Loos, 25th September 1915.

CAPTAIN ERNEST MACLAGAN WEDDERBURN, O.B.E., 2 Glenfinlas Street, Edinburgh.

Enlisted in September 1915. On General List until February 1916, when transferred to Royal Engineers. Served with Mediterranean Expeditionary Force as Meteorological Officer at General Headquarters from October 1915 till January 1916. Appointed O.C. Meteorological Section G.H.Q., Salonica, in February 1916, and was transferred to France from December 1917 till January 1918. Returned to this country as Meteorological Adviser to Ordnance Committee, and appointed Assistant Superintendent of Experiments. Awarded O.B.E. Twice mentioned in Dispatches.

**MAJOR ALEXANDER WHITE,** 22 Ann Street, Edinburgh.

Held Commission as Captain in Royal Scots and posted to 5th Royal Scots in August 1914. Thereafter promoted Major. Went to Gallipoli in July 1915. Took part in the action at Suvla Bay, and died on H.M.S. "Arcadia" from wounds received on 9th September 1915.

2ND LIEUTENANT RICHARD WHITE, 22 Rutland Street, Edinburgh.

Gazetted 2nd Lieutenant Royal Garrison Artillery 12th February 1916. Discharged on account of ill-health on 26th February 1918.

JAMES ALEXANDER WILL, 51 Castle Street, Edinburgh.

Served as Private in No. 1 Reserve M.T.D. Depot R.A.S.C. Thereafter as Warrant Officer Class 1. Attached to various M.T. Units March 1916 to February 1919.

CAPTAIN JOHN REIDFORD WISHART, 23 Rutland Street, Edinburgh. (Apprentice.)

Gazetted 2nd Lieutenant 1st Lowland Brigade Royal Field Artillery (Territorial) 14th August 1914 and attached to 51st Division. Served in Belgium and France. Wounded 3rd November 1917. Discharged owing to wounds 19th December 1917.

LIEUTENANT GEORGE MURE WOOD, 19 Alva Street, Edinburgh.

Enlisted in Royal Garrison Artillery. Promoted Lieutenant and served in Forth Coast Defences.

LIEUTENANT JOHN WILSON WYLLIE, 20 Alva Street, Edinburgh.

Received Commission as 2nd Lieutenant in the Royal Garrison Artillery on 2nd May 1917, and served at different Forts in this country. Gazetted Lieutenant in November 1918.

MAJOR THOMAS EDWIN YOUNG, Auchterarder.

Mobilised as Captain with 6th Black Watch in August 1914. Served in France with 51st Division. Promoted Major. Wounded in November 1916.

**CAPTAIN WILLIAM ALEXANDER YOUNG, M.C.,** 6 Arboretum Road, Edinburgh. (Apprentice.)

Enlisted in 9th Royal Scots in August 1914. Went to France in February 1915, and in September of that year obtained a Commission as Lieutenant in 2nd Royal Highlanders (Black Watch). Left France in November 1915 and served till the end of 1917 in Mesopotamia; thereafter in Egypt and Palestine. Was wounded in Palestine on 8th June 1918 when leading his Company in an attack against the Turks, being shot it is believed by a sniper. Died on 10th June 1918 from the effects of his wound. Was acting Captain at the time of his death. Awarded the Military Cross and twice mentioned in Dispatches.

# List of the Fallen.

## I. MEMBERS.

ROBERT BALLANTYNE ANDERSON.
JAMES DONALDSON BOSWALL.
JOHN MACKENZIE BOW.
ALEXANDER BROOK.
ARCHIBALD CAMPBELL BROWN.
RICHARD MORRIS BURNS.
GEORGE MORTON CAIRNS.
ROBERT GILLIES CAMPBELL.
HARRY CHEYNE.
GEORGE DEAS COWAN.
WILLIAM HUGH ROBERTSON DURHAM.
JAMES GILBERT HAMILTON-GRIERSON.
WILLIAM LIDDLE.
JAMES BANNERMAN LORIMER.
DAVID CAMPBELL MACEWEN.
WILLIAM ROBERT BENNY McJANNET.
KENNETH MACKENZIE.
PETER JOHN STEWART MACPHAIL.
ALEXANDER WILLIAM URQUHART MACRAE.
JAMES DOUGLAS LEITCH MELROSE.
JAMES THOMSON RANKIN MITCHELL.
JAMES GRAHAM MYLNE.
JOHN PROSSER, Jun.

JAMES PHILIP PURVES.

MATTHEW FREER RODGER.

ANDREW HAMILTON SCOTT.

CHARLES EDWARD STEWART.

JOHN WALCOT STEWART.

ALAN GRAHAM THOMSON.

THOMAS TODRICK.

JOHN DOUGLAS WATSON.

ALEXANDER WHITE.

## II. APPRENTICES.

WILLIAM SANDILANDS BROWN.

WILLIAM DERMOT COOPER.

ROWLAND FRASER.

IAN GALLETLY.

JOHN COLLIE KINMONT.

JOHN MACKINTOSH.

JOHN DONALD SHAW.

JOHN FRAZER SMITH.

JOHN JAMES ERSKINE BROWN STEWART.

WILLIAM ALEXANDER YOUNG.

# SUPPLEMENT

TO

# Roll of Honour

OF

## MEMBERS OF THE SOCIETY OF WRITERS TO HIS MAJESTY'S SIGNET, AND APPRENTICES.

1914-1919.

---

LIEUT.-COLONEL JAMES BLACK CAMERON, D.S.O., 4 Albyn Place, Edinburgh.

Commanded Lowland (City of Edinburgh) Heavy Battery, R.G.A., before the War, and mobilised as Major in Command on 4th August 1914. Proceeded to France with Battery and served in command, and also in command from time to time of various Brigades of Heavy Artillery during the fighting in France. Battles—Hooge 1915, Ancre 1916, Arras 1917, Flanders 1917, German Offensive March 1918. Awarded D.S.O., and mentioned in Dispatches. Invalided home with Trench Fever April 1918.

LIEUTENANT DAVID CORMACK, Royal Bank House, Lockerbie.

Enlisted Inns of Court O.T.C. January 1916. Received Commission as 2nd Lieutenant Royal Field Artillery Special Reserve in November 1916. Served in France from February 1917 till December 1918.

MAJOR WILLIAM COWAN, 14 Ramsay Garden, Edinburgh.

Received Commission as Captain in R.G.A. in November 1914. Served in England (in Coast Defence) 1915-17, and in France 1918; promoted Major.

COLONEL JAMES ARTHUR HOPE, 19 Charlotte Square, Edinburgh.

Raised and trained the Army Service Corps Unit for the two Scottish Horse Brigades. Thereafter acted as Military Representative to the City of Edinburgh Tribunal.

CAPTAIN DUNCAN KENNEDY, M.B.E., National Bank Buildings, Falkirk.

Gazetted Lieutenant in Royal Army Ordnance Corps on 1st September 1915. Proceeded to Salonika for service with the Salonika Expeditionary Force on 1st July 1916. Served in the Balkans till July 1919. Promoted Captain. Awarded M.B.E.

CAPTAIN ANDREW HENRY COWAN LAMB, 1 Western Terrace, Edinburgh.

Appointed Acting Paymaster, Army Pay Department, August 1915. Received Commission as Captain, A.P.D., 1st December 1918. Demobilised 22nd July 1919.

CAPTAIN HARRY HENDERSON MONTEATH, 39 Castle Street, Edinburgh.

Received Commission as 2nd Lieutenant Army Service Corps, Scottish Horse Mounted Brigade (T.F.), December 1914. Proceeded to Mesopotamia in March 1917, and served there till August 1919 as Brigade Supply Officer with 18th, and subsequently as Senior Supply Officer of 17th (Indian) Divisions. Mentioned in Dispatches.

LIEUTENANT LIONEL RUTHERFORD NICOLSON, Brough Lodge, Fetlar, Shetland.

Received Commission as Lieutenant R.N.V.R. 10th January 1915. Served first as Officer Commanding District in Shetland Section R.N.R. in Anti-Submarine Scheme. Later in H.M.S. "Implacable," Northern Patrol. Demobilised 2nd September 1919.

GILCHRIST GRAY PATTISON, 5 Clifton Terrace, Edinburgh.

Joined Army Pay Corps, attached to Headquarters, Scottish Command, Edinburgh, from 29th July 1918 to 11th April 1919, when discharged as permanently unfit for further service through nervous breakdown.

LIEUTENANT JOHN HYSLOP ROMANES, 20 Queen Street, Edinburgh.

Commissioned as Lieutenant in T.F. Reserve in July 1915, and served mainly with a Company of the Royal Defence Corps at Oldcastle, Co. Meath, Ireland, till gazetted out in April 1917, receiving thanks from War Office for services.

CAPTAIN JOHN DOUGLAS RUTHERFORD, Milness, Hoylake, Cheshire.

Joined Edinburgh University O.T.C. August 1914. Gazetted 2nd Lieutenant in Royal Army Service Corps September 1914, promoted Captain May 1915. Served in France, with 4th Division, at Arras, Ypres, and Paschendale, April to October 1917. Appointed Acting Major, August 1918.

CAPTAIN ROBERT FRANCIS SHEPHERD, 16 Charlotte Square, Edinburgh.

Received Commission as 2nd Lieutenant R.G.A. in December 1915. Promoted Lieutenant, June 1917, and Captain, August 1918. Served in this Country and at Gibraltar until October 1917, and thereafter in France until April 1919.

CAPTAIN HARRY MACDONALD SIMSON, 51 Manor Place, Edinburgh.

Enlisted in 9th Royal Scots in August 1914. Afterwards obtained a Commission and served with 52nd Lowland Divisional Train at Cape Helles, Gallipoli, from May till August 1915, and with New Zealanders at Anzac from August till September 1915; from October 1915 till August 1919 with 10th Divisional Train in Servia, Macedonia, Palestine, and Egypt.

CAPTAIN FRANCIS CLEMENT NIMMO SMITH, 86 George Street, Edinburgh.

Enlisted 5th Royal Scots August 1914. Received Commission 3rd Royal Scots October 1914. Joined 1st Royal Scots in Flanders March 1915. Served in Belgium, France, and Macedonia. Took part in Battle of Ypres, April and May 1915. Severely wounded, three places, at capture of Bala and Zir in Struma Valley, October 1916. Thereafter unfit for general service. Promoted Captain; served in United Kingdom till demobilised in May 1919.

ALEXANDER STUART WATT, 5 Circus Gardens, Edinburgh.

Attached to 2/5th Royal Scots September to November 1915. Attached to Gold Coast Regiment, West African Frontier Force, at Coomassie December 1915. Proceeded with Gold Coast Regiment in July 1916 to German East Africa. Returned to Gold Coast to refit August 1918, and transferred back from Gold Coast Regiment to Political Service in December 1918.

ACTING SERGEANT THOMAS SCOTT WELSH, 22 Castle Street, Edinburgh.

Enlisted in Royal Army Ordnance Corps. Served in France till December 1918. Promoted Acting Sergeant at Calais.

---

## *ADDITIONAL.*

LIEUTENANT WILLIAM HOLMES IVORY, 6 Albyn Place, Edinburgh.

Gazetted 2nd Lieutenant to 2/8th Battalion The Royal Scots 11th June 1915. Gazetted Lieutenant 1st July 1917. Served in France with the 5/6 Battalion The Royal Scots, 30th September 1917 to 24th December 1918.

CAPTAIN ARTHUR WALKER RUSSELL, 18 Learmonth Gardens, Edinburgh.

Commissioned as Captain 3/7th Argyll & Sutherland Highlanders, 2nd February 1915. Served with that Battalion and 5th Reserve Argyll & Sutherland Highlanders at home until April 1918, when proceeded to France. Served there with the 11th and 8th Battalions until end of June, when invalided home and was demobilised in June 1919. Also served in the Appointments Department of the Ministry of Labour, November 1918 to August 1920, when retired.

LIEUTENANT THE HONOURABLE ADAM GEORGE WATSON, 25 Melville Street, Edinburgh.

Received Commission as 2nd Lieutenant 8th (Res.) Battalion The Royal Scots, December 1914. Promoted Temporary Lieutenant March 1915. O.C. "B" Coy. 2/8th Battalion The Royal Scots May 1915 to July 1917—when disbanded. Promoted Temporary Captain June 1915—re-gazetted Lieutenant July 1917. B.E.F. attached 5/6 Battalion The Royal Scots 30th September 1917 till wounded 10th April 1918. Later attached Scottish Command in connection with Return of Prisoners of War at Leith Docks, December 1918.

www.ingramcontent.com/pod-product-compliance
Ingram Content Group UK Ltd.
Pitfield, Milton Keynes, MK11 3LW, UK
UKHW051129260726
13967UKWH00010B/2940

9 781843 424383